FOR

CALIFORNIA
AND THE
GOLD REGION DIRECT!

Mr Ken Maatz

From: Western Lithograph Company

THE WEST THAT WAS

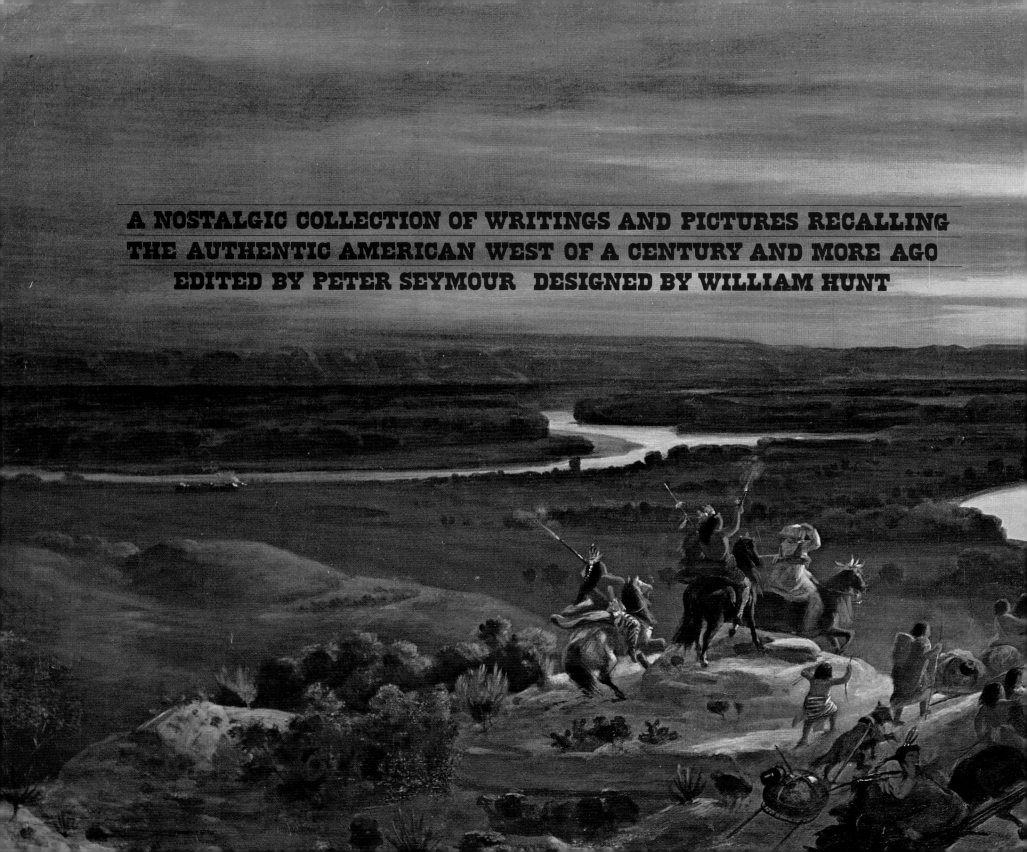

A NOSTALGIC COLLECTION OF WRITINGS AND PICTURES RECALLING
THE AUTHENTIC AMERICAN WEST OF A CENTURY AND MORE AGO
EDITED BY PETER SEYMOUR   DESIGNED BY WILLIAM HUNT

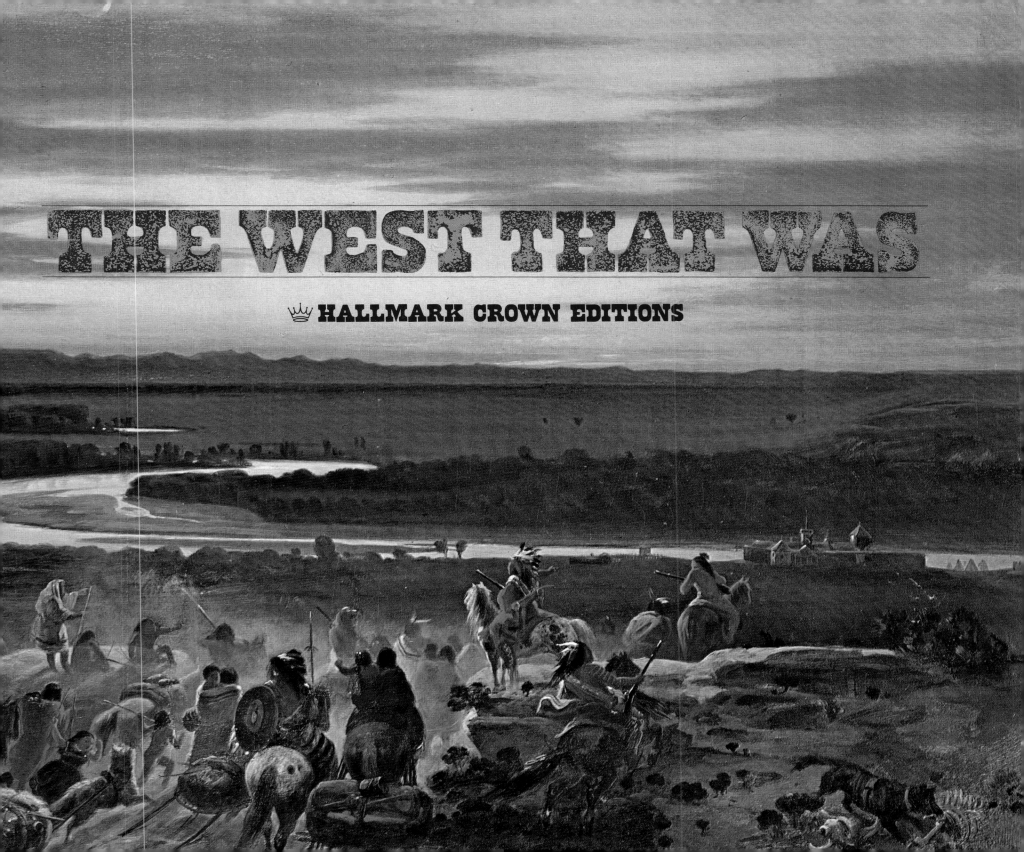

THE WEST THAT WAS

♕ HALLMARK CROWN EDITIONS

Preceding page-CARL WIMAR: *Indians Approaching Fort Union;* Washington University Gallery of Art, St. Louis, Missouri.

PICTURE CREDITS: The Bettmann Archive, pages 18, 19, 22, 23 (R), 30, 31, 35, 46, 47 (L), 48 (R), 49, 54, 55 (R), 63; Brown Brothers, pages 38, 41, 50 (R), 51, 52, 72; Culver Pictures, pages 6, 23 (L), 47 (R), 48 (L), 50 (L), 55 (L), 59, 61, 62, 70, 71, 73, 74, 75; Denver Public Library, Denver, Colorado, page 66; Jackson County Historical Society Museum, Independence, Missouri, page 7.

ACKNOWLEDGEMENTS: "The Stevens Party" excerpted and adapted from "The Smart Ones Got Through," by George R. Stewart. Reprinted by permission from *American Heritage,* June 1955. ©Copyright 1955 by American Heritage Publishing Co., Inc. "The Unsinkable Mrs. Brown" from *The Unsinkable Mrs. Brown* by Caroline Bancroft. Copyright ©1963 by Caroline Bancroft and reprinted with her permission. "The Cowboy's Lament (Once in the Saddle)" by Verne Bright taken from *A Treasury of Western Folklore* by B.A. Botkin. Copyright, 1951, by B.A. Botkin. Used by permission of Crown Publishers, Inc. "Law West of the Pecos" from *Roy Bean: Law West of the Pecos* by C.L. Sonnichsen. Copyright 1943, 1971 by C.L. Sonnichsen. Reprinted by permission of The Devin-Adair Company. "Hanging" from *A Dynasty of Western Outlaws* by Paul I. Wellman. Copyright ©1961 by Paul I. Wellman. Reprinted by permission of Doubleday & Company, Inc. "Sod House" from *The Sod House Frontier* by Dr. Everett N. Dick. Copyright 1954 by Everett N. Dick. Reprinted by permission of Johnsen Publishing Company. "The Santa Fe Trail" from *The Santa Fe Trail* by R.L. Duffus. Copyright 1958 by R.L. Duffus and reprinted with his permission. "Calamity Jane" from *Calamity Jane and the Lady Wildcats* by Duncan Aikman. Copyright 1927, ©1955 by Duncan Aikman. Reprinted by permission of Holt, Rinehart and Winston, Inc. "Buffalo Bill" from *An Autobiography of Buffalo Bill* by W.F. Cody. Copyright 1920 by Cosmopolitan Book Corporation. Copyright 1948 by William J. Garlow, Frederick H. Garlow and Jane Garlow Mallehan. Reprinted by permission of Holt, Rinehart and Winston, Inc. "Just Good Fun" from *No Life for a Lady* by Agnes Morley Cleaveland. Copyright 1941. Reprinted by permission of Houghton Mifflin Company, publisher. "Frontier Minister" by Badger Clark and "'Irregular' Doctors" from "Saddlebag Docs" by Richard Dunlop in *This Is the West,* Ed. Robert West Howard. Copyright ©1962 Robert West Howard and reprinted with his permission. "Gunfight at the O.K. Corral" from *Wyatt Earp, Frontier Marshal* by Stuart N. Lake. Copyright 1931 by Stuart N. Lake, Copyright 1964 by Carolyn Lake and reprinted with her permission. "The 'Wild' West" by Chief Luther Standing Bear from *Touch the Earth: A Self-Portrait of Indian Existence,* compiled by T.C. McLuhan. Copyright ©1971 by T.C. McLuhan. Reprinted by permission of Outerbridge and Lazard, Inc. "Black Cowboy" reprinted by permission of Quadrangle Books from *American Negro Folklore,* copyright ©1968 by J. Mason Brewer. "An Outlaw's Song," by Black Bart, Road Agent. From *Ghost Town,* by G. Ezra Dane and Beatrice J. Dane. Copyright 1941 by G. Ezra Dane and Beatrice J. Dane. Reprinted by permission of Alfred A. Knopf, Inc. "Frontier Women" from *Westward the Women,* by Nancy Wilson Ross. Copyright 1944 by Nancy Wilson Ross. Reprinted by permission of Alfred A. Knopf, Inc. "Disaster: The Donner Party" from *Diary of Patrick Breen — One of the Donner Party.* Ed. F.J. Teggart. Originally published by the University of California Press; reprinted by permission of The Regents of the University of California. "Crazy Horse" reprinted from *Crazy Horse, The Strange Man of the Oglalas: A Biography,* by Mari Sandoz, by permission of University of Nebraska Press. Copyright 1942 by Mari Sandoz. "Grub on the Trail" from *The Chisholm Trail* by Wayne Gard. Copyright 1954 by the University of Oklahoma Press and reprinted with their permission.

Set in Seldom, a variation of an American nineteenth century wood type, and in Times Roman.
Printed on Hallmark Crown Royale Book paper.
End paper and section title page illustrations by David R. Miles. Production art by Barbara Warrington.

INTRODUCTION

In the early 1800s the West had become that part of the United States beyond the Mississippi River. But it was more than just a vast and unknown territory. The West also stood for a restless, exuberant, adventurous spirit whose resounding and fluent enthusiasms encompassed the opportunities and risks, the successes and failures of man freely challenging his natural environment.

As the twentieth century arrived, however, the West had not only diminished in size — its boundaries had moved across Kansas — but, more significantly, its essential and early eloquence was rapidly falling silent.

The gold and silver mines had petered out, and communities that had sprung up overnight just as quickly became ghost towns.

Sodbusters began to fence the land where herds of cattle had roamed, and with these homesteaders and their families came the demand for law and order.

But with all the progress, with all the physical changes that came to the land, the unique spirit that had prevailed continued on in story, art and song.

Here then is a collection that recalls a golden era of Americana at its best. This is *The West That Was*.

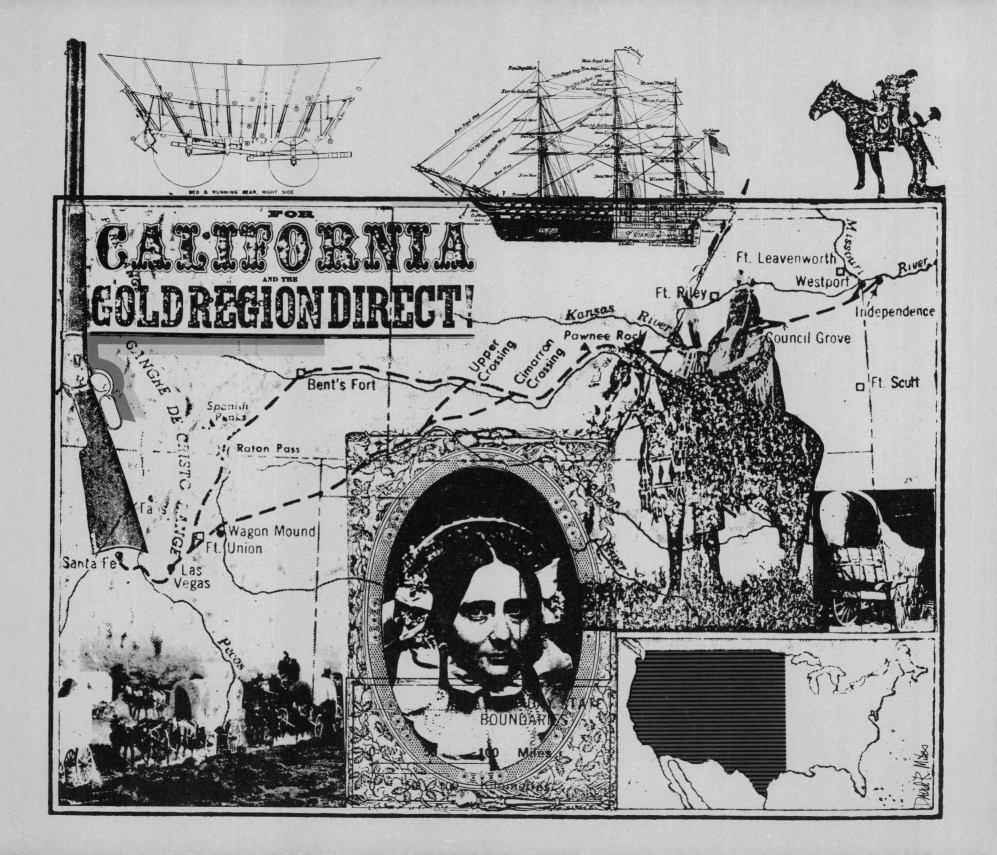

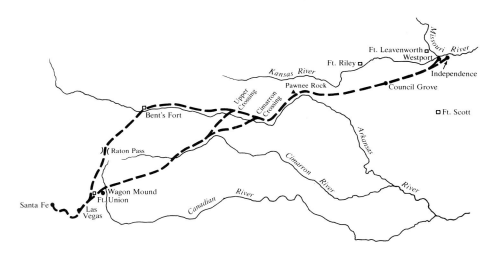

JUMPING-OFF PLACE

Organization of the wagon trains and parties of emigrants heading west was usually at Independence, Missouri. Here equipment was readied, supplies gathered, leaders chosen — with much confusion and uncertainty. The following is from The Oregon Trail *by Francis Parkman, published in 1849.*

...I rode over to Independence. The town was crowded. A multitude of shops had sprung up to furnish the emigrants and Santa Fe traders with necessaries for their journey; and there was an incessant hammering and banging from a dozen blacksmiths' sheds, where the heavy wagons were being repaired, and the horses and oxen shod. The streets were thronged with men, horses, and mules. While I was in town, a train of emigrant wagons from Illinois passed through, to join the camp on the prairie, and stopped in the principal street. A multitude of healthy children's faces were peeping out from under the covers of the wagons. Here and there a buxom damsel was seated on horseback, holding over her sunburnt face an old umbrella or a parasol, once gaudy enough, but now miserably faded. The men, very sober-looking countrymen, stood about their oxen; and as I passed I noticed three old fellows, who, with their long whips in their hands, were zealously discussing the doctrine of regeneration.

WAGON TRAIN

Jessie Applegate describes the preparation as a wagon train gets ready to move out, in the year 1843.

It is four o'clock A.M.: the sentinels on duty have discharged their rifles — the signal that the hours of sleep are over — and every wagon and tent is pouring forth its night tenants, and slow-kindling smokes begin largely to rise and float away in the morning air. Sixty men start from the corral, spreading as they make through the vast herd of cattle and horses that make a semicircle around the encampment, the most distant perhaps two miles away....

In about an hour five thousand animals are close up to the encampment, and the teamsters are busy selecting their teams and driving them inside the corral to be yoked....

From six to seven o'clock is a busy time; breakfast is to be eaten, the tents struck, the wagons loaded, and the teams yoked and brought up in readiness to be attached to their respective wagons. All know when, at seven o'clock, the signal to march sounds, that those not ready to take their proper places in the line of march must fall into the dusty rear for the day....

The women and children have taken their places in [the wagons]. The pilot (a borderer who has passed his life on the verge of civilization and has been chosen to his post of leader from his knowledge of the savage and his experience in travel through roadless wastes) stands ready, in the midst of his pioneers and aids, to mount and lead the way. Ten or fifteen young men, not to-day on duty, form another cluster. They are ready to start on a buffalo hunt, are well mounted and well armed....The cow drivers are hastening, as they get ready, to the rear of their charge to collect and prepare them for the day's march.

It is on the stroke of seven; the rushing to and fro, the cracking of whips, the loud command to oxen, and what seems to be the inextricable confusion of the last ten minutes has ceased. Fortunately every one had been found and every teamster is at his post. The clear notes of a trumpet sound in the front; the pilot and his guards mount their horses; the leading division of the wagons moves out of the encampment, and takes up the line of march; the rest fall into their places with the precision of clockwork, until the spot so lately full of life sinks back into that solitude that seems to reign over the broad plain and rushing river as the caravan draws its lazy length towards the distant El Dorado....

ALBERT BIERSTADT: *Emigrants Crossing the Plains;* National Cowboy Hall of Fame and Western Heritage Center, Oklahoma City, Oklahoma.

O.C. SELTZER: *Mother;*
Thomas Gilcrease Institute, Tulsa, Oklahoma.

FRONTIER WOMEN

Nancy Wilson Ross writes of some of the women who made the journey west, and the evidence suggests they were as hardy and courageous a group as ever lived.

The story is told of how Mrs. Longmire,…walking ahead in the midst of the untouched coastal forest carrying a babe and leading a three-year-old child, came suddenly upon a grizzled woodsman who blanched to the beard at sight of her and cried:

"Good God Almighty, woman, where did you come from? Is there any more of you? You can't get through this way. You'll have to turn back. There ain't a blade of grass for fifty miles."

But Mrs. Longmire simply walked past him with her face set to the west and, as she passed, said only: "We can't go back, we've got to go forward."…

The western trip was not, however, always dreary and discouraging. Pleasant homely pictures of life in some of the wagon trains have come down the years. A Mrs. Van Dusen, migrating from Michigan to Oregon, had only happy memories of the journey, particularly of the cosy little kitchen in her wagon…:

"On the center cross-piece was placed a little round sheet-iron stove, about the size of a three-gallon bucket, with a little tea-kettle, a boiler and frying pan. On this little stove cooking was done with great ease and satisfaction. Mrs. Van Dusen says that many times she sat in her cosy little kitchen on wheels and cleaned and cooked a bird while the wagon moved along. On cold nights their little stove made their house very comfortable. They had also a little churn in the kitchen. The milk was placed in the churn each morning and the motion of the wagon churned it, so that every evening they had fresh butter. In this way one cow furnished them with sweet milk, buttermilk, and butter daily."...

"One dare not be nervous in Oregon," wrote Sister Mary Loyola in her precise convent-bred hand, trying not to form the letters carelessly in her haste, though time was pressing.

"Especially in the woods," Loyola added, and, warming to her theme, proceeded to describe just what she meant. The Sisters often met wolves and mountain lions in broad daylight. Snakes lurked everywhere, even in the vegetable garden among the melons and cucumbers they had planted so prayerfully against the enfolding wilderness. Already Sister Aloysia, in her more sprightly style with its touch of wry humor, had written...about the "concerts" they enjoyed at the time of high flood the preceding winter; concerts consisting of the "hissing of serpents, the roaring of the mountain lions, and the howling of wolves." Yes, Sister Loyola felt that she was justified in boasting just a little to the Mother Superior. In Oregon, said she, the nuns took the killing of snakes and the chasing of wild cattle as calmly as their sheltered Belgian sisters would brush aside a fly. Only that very morning, indeed, they had had to drive away no fewer than eight wild horses.

from PIONEERS! O PIONEERS!

Come my tan-faced children,
Follow well in order, get your weapons ready,
Have you your pistols? have you your sharp-edged axes?
Pioneers! O pioneers!

For we cannot tarry here,
We must march my darlings, we must bear the brunt of danger,
We the youthful sinewy races, all the rest on us depend,
Pioneers! O pioneers!

Walt Whitman

WILLIAM TYLEE RANNEY: *Old Scout's Tale;* Thomas Gilcrease Institute, Tulsa, Oklahoma.

CHARLES RUSSELL: *Wagon Boss;* Thomas Gilcrease Institute, Tulsa, Oklahoma.

SUCCESS:
THE STEVENS PARTY

More than a year before the Donner tragedy, a group—under the leadership of Elisha Stevens—discovered the pass through the Sierra Nevada (which remains today the chief route across the area) and successfully brought the first wagons into California. Ironically the Stevens discovery became known as "Donner Pass." In the following selection, George R. Stewart recounts the last part of the Stevens journey after they have left the Oregon Trail and other known trails.

From that point they were on their own, making history by breaking trail for the forty-niners, the Central Pacific, and U.S. 40. They made it across the Forty-Mile Desert with less trouble than might have been expected, considering that they were the first. Even so, the crossing took 48 hours, and the oxen were thirst-crazed by the time they approached the cottonwoods marking the line of a stream....

Finally they came to where the river forked. Which way to go? They held "a consultation," which must

have been close to a council of desperation. It was past the middle of November—snow two feet deep now, high mountain crags in view ahead, oxen footsore and gaunt, food low, womenfolk getting scared. But they were good men and staunch....

[They] worked out the plan, and it came out in the end as what we would call today a calculated risk, with a certain hedging of the bets. Leave five wagons below the pass at what is now called Donner Lake, and three young men with them, volunteers, to build a cabin and guard the wagons and goods through the winter. Take six wagons ahead over the pass, and with them the main body including all the mothers and children. Up the other fork of the river, send a party of two women and four men, all young, well-mounted and well-armed,

prepared to travel light and fast and live off the country. Unencumbered they can certainly make it through somewhere; when they get to Sutter's Fort, they can have help sent back, if necessary.

So Captain Stevens and the main body took the six wagons ahead to the west, and with a heave and a ho, in spite of sheer granite ledges and ever-deepening snow, they hoisted those wagons up the pass, which is really not a pass so much as the face of a mountain....

Beyond the pass, some days' journey, they got snowed in, but by that time they were over the worst. On Yuba River they built a cabin to winter it out, and Elizabeth Yuba Murphy was born there. Eventually all of them, including E.Y.M., together with the wagons, got safely through to Sutter's [Fort]....

These are the ones who discovered the pass and took the wagons over, who kept out of emergencies or had the wit and strength to overcome them, who did not make a good story by getting into trouble, but made history by keeping out of trouble.

DISASTER: THE DONNER PARTY

Of the 89 men, women, and children in the Donner party who headed for California in July 1846, only 47 survived. Snowed in before they could cross the mountains, the group managed to build cabins. As the winter progressed, however, they began to die of starvation. Following are excerpts from the diary of Patrick Breen, a survivor.

1847 Jan. Tuesd 26   Cleared up yesterday   to day fine & pleasant, wind S. in hopes we are done with snow storms…provisions geting very scant people geting weak liveing on short allowance of hides.

Weds 27th   Began to snow yesterday & still continues to sleet   Mrs. Keyber here this morning   Lewis Suitor she says died three days ago Keysburg sick & Lanthrom lying in bed the whole of his time   dont have fire enough to cook their hides.

Satd. 30th   Fine pleasant morning begining to thaw in the sun John & Edwd. went to Graves this morning   the Graves seized on Mrs Reids goods untill they would be paid also took the hides that she & family had to live on, she got two peices of hides from there & the ballance they have taken you may know from these proceedings what our fare is in camp   there is nothing to be got by hunting yet perhaps there soon will. God send it Amen….

Feb. Mond. 15. Morning cloudy untill 9 o clock then cleared off wam & sunshine   wind W.   Mrs Graves refusd. to give Mrs Reid any hides put Suitors pack hides on her shanty would not let her have them says if I say it will thaw it then will not,   she is a case.

Mond 22nd   The Californians started this morning 24 in number some in a very weak state   fine morning   wind S.W. for the 3 last days   Mrs Keyburg started & left Keysburg here unable to go   I burried Pikes child this morning in the snow   it died 2 days ago….

Tuesd. 23   Shot Towser to day & dressed his flesh   Mrs Graves came here this morning to borrow meat dog or ox they think I have meat to spare but I know to the contrary they have plenty hides I live principally on the same.

Thursd. 25th   Mrs Murphy says the wolves are about to dig up the dead bodies at her shanty, the nights are too cold to watch them, we hear them howl.

Frid 26th   Marthas jaw swelled with the toothache; hungry times in camp, plenty hides but the folks will not eat them we eat them with a tolerable good apetite. Thanks be to Almighty God. Amen   Mrs Murphy said here yesterday that thought she would commence on Milt. & eat him. I dont that she has done so yet, it is distressing   The Donnos told the California folks that they commence to eat the dead people 4 days ago, if they did not succeed that day or next in finding their cattle then under ten or twelve feet of snow & did not know the spot or near it, I suppose they have done so ere this time.

THE SANTA FE TRAIL

Long before the white man, Indians used the route that became known as the Santa Fe Trail. In the 1800s it was the key to exploration, trade, and settlement in the Southwest. R. L. Duffus captures the spirit of the Trail.

The wilderness was laid out on a scale that dazed and delighted eyes used to the pocket landscapes of New England. You passed from the lush prairies to the short-grass country, from that to burning deserts. You came upon milky rivers half sunken in their shining sands. You saw mountains glistening like polished silver in the remote distances, or hanging like faint clouds above the horizon. Day after day, as you travelled your fifteen or twenty miles between sunrise and sunset, the horizon slowly altered. You slept under the bright stars, or huddled in your tent, or under the shelter of your wagons, while thunder-storms beat down with dreadful violence. You shot elk and deer. The wild fowl rose in clouds from the water courses. The buffalo crossed your path in uncounted hordes, swathed in moving clouds of dust. Indians hovered on all sides....

You met Mexicans riding beside the caravans, packers and trappers coming in with furs....

You suffered from heat, thirst, mosquitos, gnats; you ate rigorously plain food and slept on the hardest of beds; but if you were young and in health you attained at last to an inexpressible hardihood and buoyancy.

CROSSING THE PLAINS (1878)

What great yoked brutes with briskets low,
With wrinkled necks like buffalo,
With round, brown, liquid, pleading eyes,
That turn'd so slow and sad to you,
That shone like love's eyes soft with tears,
That seem'd to plead, and make replies,
The while they bow'd their necks and drew
The creaking load; and looked at you.
Their sable briskets swept the ground,
Their cloven feet kept solemn sound.

Two sullen bullocks led the line,
Their great eyes shining bright like wine;
Two sullen captive kings were they,
That had in time held herds at bay,
And even now they crush'd the sod
With stolid sense of majesty,
And stately stepp'd and stately trod,
As if 't were something still to be
Kings even in captivity.

Joaquin Miller

SAILING WEST

Before the transcontinental railroads, many people traveled from the East to West Coast by ship; some around the Horn, and others by crossing on land at Panama and picking up a second ship. This selection, written by a Mr. Hubert Bancroft in 1852, pictures the first port of call on the Pacific leg—Acapulco.

Scarcely does the steamer come to anchor before it is surrounded by canoes laden with fruit, which come swarming from various parts of the shore, and naked swimmers ready to begin their aquatic gymnastics....While the steamer is taking on coals, cattle, fowls, fruit, and water, which occupies several hours, you may if you like go ashore in a boat and visit the town, less than a mile distant, in a recess of the bay. Near the landing, and on the shady side of the plaza, you will find spread out on tables and on the ground fruit and fancy shellwork which you are solicited to purchase.... As you walk along, a charming pensive-eyed senorita throws over your head a necklace, at the same time saying it is a present, but should you let it remain you will not have gone far before the coffee-colored

beauty turns up and desires a present in return....At night, in the absence of the moon, the town is lighted by lanterns hung out at the doors. Contentment and happiness reign; the women, some of them quite beautiful, gather fruit, and make and sell shell-work; the men lounge in shady nooks, smoke, and sip aguardiente, and naked children suck oranges, munch bananas, and roll in the dirt.

SANTA FE: END OF THE TRAIL

At the conclusion of the long trek, the wagon trains passed in review before the residents of Santa Fe. This account of that welcomed occasion by Josiah Gregg was published in the 1840s.

I doubt whether the first sight of the walls of Jerusalem were beheld by the crusaders with much more tumultuous and soul-enrapturing joy....The wagoners were by no means free from excitement on this occasion. Informed of the "ordeal" they had to pass they had spent the previous morning in "rubbing up," and now they were prepared, with clean faces, sleek-combed hair and their choicest Sunday suit, to meet the "fair eyes" of glistening black that were sure to stare at them as they passed. There was yet another preparation to be made in order to "show off" to advantage. Each wagoner must tie a brand-new cracker to the lash of his whip, for on driving through the streets and the *plaza publica* everyone strives to outvie his comrade in the dexterity with which he flourishes his favorite brand of authority.

WILLIAM HAHN: *Sacramento Railroad Station;*
M.H. de Young Memorial Museum, San Francisco, California.

CALIFORNY, WE'RE HERE!

A man named J.H. Beadle expresses his enthusiasm on reaching California in the 1870s.

Well, we was into Californy at last, an' it looked like heaven to me. There was big trees, an' the wind blowin' soft away up in their tops; an' the pretty clear streams down the mountain side an' through the gulches made music all day. In some places the air was jist sweet that blowed out o' the pine woods, an' week after week the sky was so blue, an' the air so soft, it seemed like a man could stand anything. An' no matter how hard you worked in the day, or how hot it was, it was always so cool an' nice at night; you could sleep anywheres—on the ground or on a pile o' limbs, in the house or out o' doors, an' never catch cold.

GOLD!

SIMPSON'S 1848 CALIFORNIA GUIDE
WITH THE MAP

In late January 1848, Jim Marshall, who was working on Captain Sutter's new sawmill by the American River in the Sierra foothills, found gold in the mill's tailrace. Following are excerpts from Marshall's own description of the event as recorded by Charles B. Gillespie.

One morning in January,—it was a clear, cold morning; I shall never forget that morning—as I was taking my usual walk along the race after shutting off the water, my eye was caught with the glimpse of something shining in the bottom of the ditch. There was about a foot of water running then. I reached my hand down and picked it up; it made my heart thump, for I was certain it was gold....

In about a week's time after the discovery I...showed it to Mr. Sutter, who at once declared it was gold, but thought with me that it was greatly mixed with some other metal....After hunting over the whole fort [Sutter's Fort] and borrowing from some of the men, we got three dollars and a half in silver, and with a small pair of scales we soon ciphered it out that there was no silver nor copper in the gold, but that it was entirely pure.

This fact being ascertained, we thought it our best policy to keep it as quiet as possible till we should have finished our mill. But there was a great number of disbanded Mormon soldiers in and about the fort, and when they came to hear of it, why it just spread like wildfire, and soon the whole country was in a bustle. I had scarcely arrived at the mill again till several persons appeared with pans, shovels, and hoes, and those that had not iron picks had wooden ones, all anxious to fall to work and dig up our mill; but this we would not permit. As fast as one party disappeared another would arrive, and sometimes I had the greatest kind of trouble to get rid of them. I sent them all off in different directions, telling them about such and such places, where I was certain there was plenty of gold if they would only take the trouble of looking for it....

The second place where gold was discovered was in a gulch near the Mountaineer House, on the road to Sacramento. The third place was on a bar on the South Fork of the American River a little above the junction of the Middle and South forks. The diggings at Hangtown were discovered next by myself, for we all went out for a while as soon as our job was finished. The Indians next discovered the diggings at Kelsay's, and thus in a very short time we discovered that the whole country was but one bed of gold.

A miner named L.M. Shaeffer describes life in Hawkinsville, "with a population of about one thousand men; not a single woman...."

A neighbor offered me the use of his tent and board at nine dollars a week..., the bill of fare to consist of salt pork of questionable age, musty crackers and tip-top coffee, provided somebody knew how to make it. However, I relished the food and never enjoyed better health....

With only a knife, broken pick and pan, did I, day after day, search for the glittering metal, secreted amid rocks, crevices and dirt. The general custom was to dig down until a stratum of earth was reached, which indicated the presence of gold. The earth was then shoveled into the box on top the rocker, water was constantly poured upon it, whilst the rocker was shaken to and fro; at night that left in the bottom of the cradle was carefully scooped up, and the profits of the day's labor soon known.

THE COWBOY
AND
THE INDIAN

SONG

Oh, bury me out on the lone prairie
In a narrow grave just six by three,
Where the wild coyotes will howl o'er me;
Oh, bury me out on the lone prairie.

Author Unknown

O.C. SELTZER: *Horse Wrangler;*
Thomas Gilcrease Institute, Tulsa, Oklahoma.

"SO YOU WANT TO BE A COW-BOY!"

In memoirs published in 1893, W.S. James, himself a cowboy, writes about the "dudes" who came from the East to establish themselves in cattle country.

One circumstance that I recall was a young man who came to Texas in '82; he had in cash $30,000 to invest in a ranch. He landed in a western town, met some of the boys, and made known his intentions; he also made free to state that he was "onto" cow-boys, but wished to thoroughly learn the ropes, etc.; so they took him in hand, learned first his ideas concerning the business, blowed him in for $100, for an old stove-up pony, a sixty-five dollar saddle, a pair of flashy red blankets, spurs, quirt, rope and leggings, cow-boy hat, two six-shooters and a long keen knife; after tanking him up on red liquor they started him out to paint the town red, taking care all the while to keep their own necks out of the halter, which a cow-boy knows just how to do....

...Next morning when he awoke, he was all alone, horse, saddle, blankets and everything he had started with, gone. They had made him drunk and robbed him of everything while he was asleep, and were in hiding to see the effect on him. He looked all around, and then hit the road and began to cut dirt for town, a sadder but wiser man. Some of the boys followed him at a safe distance with his outfit, and when they saw him get in a farmer's wagon, they surrounded him, beat him to town and hitched his horse where he could find him when he came in. The man of whom he bought the horse went to him and gave him back his money, took the old horse off his hands and gave him five hundred dollars worth of good advice in a few words. That young man, unlike many who started just as he did, took the advice, went to work, learned the cattle business and afterward became a reasonably good cattleman, but like a great many of the more visionary among the boys went under in the great rise and fall of cattle from 1880 to 1885.

O.C.SELTZER: *Cattle Rustler;* Thomas Gilcrease Institute, Tulsa, Oklahoma.

O.C.SELTZER: *Bronco Buster;* Thomas Gilcrease Institute, Tulsa, Oklahoma.

CHARLES RUSSELL: *Jerked Down;*
Thomas Gilcrease Institute, Tulsa, Oklahoma.

FREDERIC REMINGTON: *The Arizona Cowboy;*
National Cowboy Hall of Fame and Western Heritage Center,
Oklahoma City, Oklahoma.

THE COW-BOY

Historian Paul Horgan portrays the cowboy as "the last of the clearly original types of Western American to draw his general tradition and character from the kind of land he worked in, and the kind of work he did."

In dealing with cows through the consent of his horse, the cow-boy needed to know much of the nature of both animals. Through experience he learned to anticipate the behavior of cattle, and to judge the effect upon them of every stimulus. He saw that the laws that governed them were the laws of the crowd; and he developed extraordinary skill in handling great crowds of cattle at a time. His horse, broken to riding, and subject to his will, he had to know as an individual creature, and dominate relentlessly its nature by turns sensitive, stubborn, and gentle. Living with these two animal natures, the cow-boy seemed to acquire as his own certain of their traits, almost as though to be effective at living and working with them, he must open his own animal nature to theirs and through sympathy resemble them. If he could be as simple as a cow, he could also be as stubborn; as fearless as a wild mustang, and as suspicious of the unfamiliar; as incurious as an individual bull, and as wild to run with a crowd when attracted.

JUST GOOD FUN

Life was hard on the trail and on the ranch, and so were the jokes and pranks, as recalled in the book No Life for a Lady *by Agnes Morley Cleaveland.*

Of course, there were endless practical jokes. Stock among them was that of rattling a set of chain traces and yelling "Whoa!" close to the head of a sleeping man, who very reasonably thinks the chuck-wagon team is stampeding and is about to run over him. His exit from his bedroll is explosive.

Seeing to it that the other fellow's horse pitches is routine on a frosty morning. Horses' humor is no better than that of their human brethren on cold mornings, and any unexpected happening will set them off. So yell and throw your hat under the feet of your neighbor's horse just as he mounts, and the chances are you'll have a nice little rodeo right then and there. It is not difficult to understand why we had so few gentle horses. We had so few gentle people!

According to James H. Cook, whether the food served to the trail hands on a cattle drive was any good or not, a cheerful cook was always welcome.

...A camp cook could do more toward making life pleasant for those about him than any other man in the outfit. A good-natured, hustling cook meant a lot to a trail boss. A cheery voice ringing out at daybreak, shouting, "Roll out there, fellers, and hear the little birdies sing their praises to God!" or "Arise and shine and give God the glory!" would make the most crusty waddy grin as he crawled out to partake of his morning meal—even when he was extremely short of sleep.

Wayne Gard describes what cowboys generally thought of the grub.

...The trail hands, although usually "hungry enough to eat a saddle blanket" and not choosey about food, might find the fare monotonous and complain in song:

Oh, it's bacon and beans 'most every day—
I'd as soon be eatin' prairie hay.

At meals on the trail, the men, often leaving their hats on, helped themselves to food and coffee. Then, with legs crossed, they sat on the prairie and ate their fill. When through, they dropped their tin plates, cups, and cutlery in the dishpan or tub, the "wreck pan." If they didn't like the food, they seldom dared complain within hearing of the cook. But, after a hard day in the saddle, almost any grub was likely to taste good. Most of the trail men preferred the rough cow-camp fare to that of town restaurants, whose "wasp-nest" bread they rated a poor substitute for fluffy sour-dough biscuits.

CHARLES RUSSELL: *When Guns Speak Death Settles Dispute;* Thomas Gilcrease Institute, Tulsa, Oklahoma.

LETTING OFF STEAM

Cowboy antics like the ones related here by Theodore Roosevelt had a lot to do with the West being characterized as wild.

One evening at Medora a cowboy spurred his horse up the steps of a rickety "hotel" piazza into the barroom, where he began firing at the clock, the decanters, etc., the bartender meanwhile taking one shot at him, which missed. When he had emptied his revolver he threw down a roll of banknotes on the counter, to pay for the damage he had done, and galloped his horse out through the door, disappearing in the darkness with loud yells to a rattling accompaniment of pistol-shots interchanged between himself and some passer-by who apparently began firing out of pure desire to enter into the spirit of the occasion — for it was the night of the Fourth of July, and all the country round about had come into town for a spree.

O.C. SELTZER: *Bar Keep;*
Thomas Gilcrease Institute, Tulsa, Oklahoma.

O.C. SELTZER: *Dance Hall Girl;*
Thomas Gilcrease Institute, Tulsa, Oklahoma.

FREDERIC REMINGTON: *Stampeded by Lightning;* Thomas Gilcrease Institute, Tulsa, Oklahoma.

Under this sod lies a great bucking hoss;
There never lived a cowboy he couldn't toss.
His name was Midnight—his coat black as coal.
If there is a hoss heaven, please God, rest his soul!

On the Grave
At National Cowboy Hall of Fame,
Oklahoma City

BLACK COWBOY

Following the Civil War, Negroes moved in large numbers into the mainstream of Western life as soldiers, miners, settlers, and especially as cowboys (such as Nat Love, shown at far right). J. M. Brewer recalls:

Mama did day work in town sometimes for a ranch owner by the name of Dillard Fant. Colonel Fant and his family thought a whole lot of Mama, so when she asked him to give me a job as a cowhand on one of his ranches he said "All right, Martha (that was Mama's name), I'll give the boy a job if you want him to have it." So Colonel Fant loaded me on a wagon one Saturday morning with some more Goliad men he had hired as cowhands and carried me out to one of his ranches....

Colonel Fant had a contract with the government to furnish beef for the Indians in the Indian Territory, so he employed about a hundred Negroes and Mexicans to drive his herds up the trail every year or work the cattle he sold and shipped by train to Ardmore, Oklahoma.

The year I started working for Colonel Fant was 1887, and I didn't get very far up the trail that first trip. We had barely got started; the fact of it is we hardly reached Live Oak County when our whole herd was sold to another ranch owner by the name of George West. So instead of using our crew to drive cattle up the trail that year, Colonel Fant had us to build a water tank on one of his ranches in Live Oak County. We started building the tank in April and finished it on August 12, but a cyclone came along on August 13, and it was blown to pieces—over a hundred days of hard work by twenty-five men wrecked in just a few minutes.

FREDERIC REMINGTON: *An Indian Trapper;*
Amon Carter Museum of Western Art, Fort Worth, Texas.

THE "WILD" WEST

Chief Luther Standing Bear of the Oglala band of Sioux speaks:

We did not think of the great open plains, the beautiful rolling hills, and winding streams with tangled growth, as "wild." Only to the white man was nature a "wilderness" and only to him was the land "infested" with "wild" animals and "savage" people. To us it was tame. Earth was bountiful and we were surrounded with the blessings of the Great Mystery. Not until the hairy man from the east came and with brutal frenzy heaped injustices upon us and the families we loved was it "wild" for us. When the very animals of the forest began fleeing from his approach, then it was that for us the "Wild West" began.

HENRY F. FARNY: *Indian Camp;* Cincinnati Art Museum

CRAZY HORSE

As a boy — light of skin, with soft, pale hair — he was called "Curly." He came from a long line of holy men, wise and quiet, fine hunters and brave warriors — but never ones to seek out honors. Yet glory was to be thrust upon him in the sad battle of the Indian tribes against the overwhelming tides of the white man's push west. His father was called Crazy Horse, and at age 17, after his first real battle in which he was slightly wounded, the name was conferred upon him.

The following selection by Mari Sandoz describes the Great Teton Council in 1857, and his ceremonial naming.

For the first time Curly saw the great ones of the northern Lakotas that he had been hearing about at the winter fires: old Four Horns, the Hunkpapa, and his warrior nephew, Sitting Bull; Long Mandan of the Two Kettles; Crow Feather of the No Bows. And standing beside these some from his own country still seemed great to the young Oglala: their own chief, Man Afraid; Lone Horn of the North, the Minneconjou; and the rising men like Red Cloud and Lone Horn's seven-foot warrior son, Touch the Clouds. Spotted Tail was there, too, known everywhere as a brave man, but now as one returned from the death scaffold, older, quieter, and talking for peace even here. Not that he liked the white man's peace, it seemed, but because the whites were so many.

There was something else that Curly and many much older than he had never seen before, the seven great camps of the Tetons together — Oglala, Brule, Minneconjou, No Bows, Blackfoot, Two Kettles and Hunkpapa — all in the sacred circle. It was really the way Crazy Horse had told his son. As their own Hunkpatilas were one of the seven bands of the Oglalas, the Oglalas were one of the seven camps of the Tetons. And bigger yet, all the Tetons together here were one of the seven great council fires of the Lakota nation. It made the boy feel a part of something holy to think of the repetition of this sacred number, each one a part of seven in a circle which was one of seven in a greater circle, and that a part of the greatest, the whole.

Ahh-h, it was plain now that the Lakotas were still the same as in the old days, everyone was saying as the chiefs came in a great row from the last council, walking firm together, their moccasins strong on their earth. They had vowed resistance to every white man who pushed in anywhere on Teton lands. They would get guns and powder; they would stick together, for they were many.

Young Curly saw them so, and in him grew again the feeling of power he knew that first day when he looked upon the great camp. Let the whites be even as many as his uncle said. Some day the Lakotas would rise as a storm cloud piling high over the Black Hills and, sweeping out over the plains, would shake all the earth as far as the muddy waters of the Missouri.

Perhaps he, still called by his childhood name of Curly, would live long enough to see this done....

The next morning [after Curly's first real battle] he still felt bad and so he lay still on his side of the lodge, so still that even his brother thought him sleeping. As his people got up they went out quietly, and finally young Curly slept. When the sun stood almost straight up, he awoke and was given a horn spoon of soup. Then Crazy Horse came in and took his ceremonial blanket from its case, the one with the beaded band across the middle showing all the sacred things of his holy vision. With this blanket about him, his braids long and fur-wrapped on his breast, the father walked slowly through the village, making a song as he went, singing it so all might hear:

My son has been against the people of unknown tongue.
He has done a brave thing;
For this I give him a new name, the name of his father, and of many fathers before him —
I give him a great name
I call him Crazy Horse.

And behind the father came all those of the village who wished to honor the young man among them who had done a brave deed. By the time they came to the lodge where the boy sat, there was a mighty double line of the people until it seemed that everybody was walking in it: young men, old men, great men, wise ones, and all the women and the children too, all singing and laughing.

Then there was feasting and dancing all that day and late into the night, for among the Oglalas there was a new warrior, a warrior to be known by the great name of Crazy Horse.

FREDERIC REMINGTON: *Indian Warfare;* Thomas Gilcrease Institute, Tulsa, Oklahoma.

COCHISE

For years the great chieftain Cochise led Indians on the warpath. Then in the 1870s, Major General O.O. Howard, accompanied by a white man named Jeffords who knew Cochise and the Apache ways, undertook a peace mission. Negotiations went slowly, and Howard lived among the Indians for some time. Finally a great tribal council was held, which Howard recalls:

The evening after the council a strange ceremony for consulting the spirits was observed by the Indians. It took place on a separate plateau near my bivouac. I was not to be present at the beginning of the performance. I could, however, hear the muffled sound of voices of a multitude of women apparently imitating the low moaning of the wind. Then all—men and women— sang with ever increasing volume of sound, and the women's voices rose higher and higher. It was a wild, weird performance.

In due time the roughest-appearing Apache that I had ever seen, tall and muscular, his long hair hanging in braids down his back, ran toward me. His manner was not as fierce as his appearance would indicate, for he now spoke gently and invited me and all our white men to join the band on the plateau. Arriving there we sat outside the women's circle—the male Indians being seated within it. As soon as the singing ceased the men kept on talking, but without rising. An authoritative voice now silenced all the others. It was Cochise speaking in a mournful recitative. More than once I heard him use Jeffords' sobriquet, "Stag-li-to," meaning Redbeard. Our whole case was evidently being discussed at the meeting. Those were solemn moments to us, for we could not determine on which side of the Styx their superstitions might land us.

Fortunately, the spirits were on our side. Their answer to the Indian incantation was rendered through Cochise, who said: "Hereafter the white man and the Indian are to drink of the same water, eat of the same bread, and be at peace." I felt that the object of my mission was now accomplished.

PEACE

In 1877 the military conquest of the
American Indians was more or less
complete with the surrender of Chief
Joseph of the Nez Percé tribe. Here
are the stirring words of Chief
Joseph at the surrender.

Hear me, my warriors; my heart is sick and sad.
Our chiefs are killed, the old men are all dead.
It is cold, and we have no blankets; the little
children are freezing to death. Hear me, my warriors;
my heart is sick and sad. From where the sun now
stands I will fight no more forever!

FREDERIC REMINGTON: *Battle of War Bonnet Creek;*
Thomas Gilcrease Institute, Tulsa, Oklahoma.

OUTLAWS
AND
HEROES

"CALAMITY JANE"

Colorful names for colorful characters — the West was full of them, and women were no exception. About the most famous of the latter was Calamity Jane. How she came by this designation is uncertain, but according to historian Duncan Aikman:

She rolled it on her tongue, she screeched it, tumbled it out with a mouthful of oaths in melodramatic contralto, and obviously loved it. "I'm Calamity Jane and this drink's on the house," she howled at hesitating Wyoming bartenders. "I'm Calamity Jane. Get to hell out of here and let me alone," were her first proud words when awakened from a somewhat unlady-like stupor in a Cheyenne woodshed. "I'm Calamity Jane and I sleep when and where I damn please," she informed a conventional young man from the east who returned to his quarters in an impeccable Cheyenne rooming house one Sunday afternoon in 1873 to find her stretched out in full bullwhacker's toggery on his otherwise inviolate couch. "Calam's here," the crowd roared in the Cheyenne dance house and the intermission gayeties of McDaniel's Theater. "You bet Calam's here," would come back the squaw-like war-whoop coupled with invocations to the sons of all the indignities. "Now let her rip."

"WILD BILL" HICKOCK

This verbal sketch of "Wild Bill" Hickock comes from My Life on the Plains *by General George A. Custer. The book was published before his death at the Battle of the Little Big Horn.*

"Wild Bill" was a strange character, just the one which a novelist might gloat over. He was a Plainsman in every sense of the word, yet unlike any other of his class....

His hair and complexion were those of the perfect blond. The former was worn in uncut ringlets falling carelessly over his powerfully formed shoulders. Add to this figure a costume blending the immaculate neatness of the dandy with the extravagant taste and style of the frontiersman, and you have Wild Bill, then as now, the most famous scout on the Plains....

His skill in the use of the rifle and pistol was unerring; while his deportment was exactly the opposite of what might be expected from a man of his surroundings. It was entirely free from all bluster or bravado. He seldom spoke of himself unless requested to do so. His conversation, strange to say, never bordered either on the vulgar or blasphemous. His influence among the frontiersmen was unbounded, his word was law; and many are the personal quarrels and disturbances which he has checked among his comrades by his simple announcement that "this has gone far enough," if need be followed by the ominous warning that when persisted in or renewed the quarreller "must settle it with me."

"BUFFALO BILL"

William F. Cody tells how he came to be called "Buffalo Bill."

Having heard of my experience and success as a buffalo hunter, Goddard Brothers, who had the contract for feeding the men [who were building the Kansas Pacific Railroad], made me a good offer to become their hunter. They said they would require about twelve buffaloes a day—twenty-four hams and twelve humps, as only the hump and hindquarters of each animal were utilized. The work was dangerous. Indians were riding all over that section of the country, and my duties would require me to journey from five to ten miles from the railroad every day in order to secure the game, accompanied by only one man with a light wagon to haul the meat back to camp. I demanded a large salary...five hundred dollars a month, agreeing on my part to supply them with all the meat they wanted....

...It was not long before I acquired a considerable reputation, and it was at this time that the title "Buffalo

Bill" was conferred upon me by the railroad hands. Of this title, which has stuck to me through life, I have never been ashamed.

During my engagement as hunter for the company, which covered a period of eighteen months, I killed 4,280 buffaloes and had many exciting adventures with the Indians, including a number of hair-breadth escapes.

50

AN OUTLAW'S SONG

Here I lay me down to sleep
  To wait the coming morrow,
Perhaps success, perhaps defeat
  And everlasting sorrow.

Let come what will, I'll try it on,
  My condition can't be worse,
And if there's money in that box
  'Tis money in my purse.

This is my way to get money and bread,
  When I have a chance why should I refuse it.
I'll not need either when I'm dead,
  And I only tax those who are able to lose it.

So blame me not for what I've done,
  I don't deserve your curses;
And if for some cause I must be hung,
  Let it be for my verses.

Black Bart, Road Agent

PORTRAIT OF AN OUTLAW

In the Kansas City Times, *May 12, 1872, there appeared a description of William Clarke Quantrill, leader of the dreaded guerrillas who terrorized Kansas following the Civil War.*

Quantrill might be likened to a blond Apollo of the prairies. His eyes were very blue, soft and winning. Looking at his face, one might say there is the face of a student....If there is a race born without fear, Quantrill belonged to it....In his war-life which was one long, long merciless crusade, he exhibited all the qualities of cunning, skill, nerve, daring, physical endurance, remorseless cruelty, abounding humor, insatiable revenge, a courage that was sometimes cautious to excess and sometimes desperate to temerity.

"Hear ye! Hear ye! This honorable court's now in session; and if any galoot wants a snort afore we start, let him step up to the bar and name his pizen...."

Judge Roy Bean

LAW WEST OF THE PECOS

The incredible "judge" Roy Bean spent part of his varied career, around 1880, in a railroad tent town called Vinegaroon, near the Rio Grande and Pecos rivers. It was the largest— and considered to be the wickedest— place around. Here Roy Bean opened a saloon and dispensed a self-styled justice. C.L. Sonnichsen recreates the scene.

"Law West of the Pecos" he called himself—and people thought he was joking. Law and order in that God-forsaken hell hole? Why half the badmen in Texas were on the dodge out there. A peace officer wouldn't last overnight in that climate, and what use would there be for a judge?

Why hell, man, the United States Army couldn't clean it up!

"Maybe so," said Roy Bean. "Court will come to order."...

The horse-thief story shows how this rugged frontier justice operated. One day a rancher brought in a sorry-looking specimen and lined him up before the Judge.

"What's he charged with?"

"Stealing horses, Judge."

"Whose horses?"

"Mine."

"You sure about it?"

"Caught him at it. He was drawing them across the ford."

"Who nicked his ear?"

"I did when he didn't stop."

"Too bad you're such a damn poor shot."

Judge Bean thereupon took the man's gun away and advised him with deep earnestness, "Now you get the hell out of here and if you're ever caught in these parts again you'll be strung up pronto."

The horse thief disappeared down the track and as far as Roy was concerned justice had been done. The horses had been recovered. The thief had a good chance of getting back to civilization, though his lack of horse and gun complicated his problem considerably. At least the man was gone; the county had no expense over him; and the ranger force was still intact. Maybe it wasn't good law but it was good common sense.

GUNFIGHT AT THE O. K. CORRAL

Tombstone, Arizona—October 26, 1881: A showdown came to a head between a gang of outlaws and Wyatt Earp (above, third from left), his brothers Virgil and Morgan, and Doc Holliday. The outlaw group—Ike and Billy Clanton, Tom and Frank McLowery, and Billy Claiborne—had stationed themselves at the O.K. Corral, with strategic views of the streets that the Earps and Holliday would have to take to reach their homes. It was fight or run. Stuart N. Lake unfolds the legendary scene.

Along Fourth Street the Earp party had been two abreast, Wyatt and Virgil in the lead, with Virgil on the outside, Morgan behind him, and Doc Holliday back of Wyatt. Each sensed instinctively what could happen if they rounded the corner of Fly's Photograph Gallery abruptly in close order, and at the street intersection they deployed catercorner to walk four abreast, in the middle of the road.

Half a dozen persons who saw the four men on their journey down Fremont Street have described them. The recollections agree strikingly in detail. No more grimly portentous spectacle had been witnessed in Tombstone.

The three stalwart, six-foot Earps— each with the square jaw of his clan set hard beneath his flowing, tawny mustache and his keen blue eyes alert under the wide brim of a high-peaked, black Stetson—bore out their striking resemblance, even in their attire; dark trousers drawn outside the legs of black, high-heeled boots, long-skirted, square-cut, black coats then in frontier fashion, and white, soft-collared shirts with black string-ties to accentuate the purpose in their lean, bronzed faces. Doc Holliday was some two inches shorter than his three companions, but his stature was heightened by cadaverousness, the flapping black overcoat and the black sombrero above his hollow cheeks. Holliday's blond mustache was as long and as sweeping as any, but below it those who saw him have sworn Doc had his lips pursed, whistling softly. As the distance to the O.K. Corral lessened, the four men spread their ranks as they walked....

The Earps moved in....Virgil Earp was well into the corral, Wyatt about opposite Billy Clanton and Frank McLowery, Morg[an] facing Tom. Not a gun had been drawn. Wyatt Earp was determined there'd be no gunplay that the outlaws did not begin.

"You men are under arrest. Throw up your hands," Virgil Earp commanded....

Frank McLowery dropped his hand to his six-gun and snarled defiance in short, ugly words. Tom McLowery, Billy Clanton, and Billy Claiborne followed concerted suit.

"Hold on!" Virgil Earp shouted, instinctively throwing up his right hand, which carried Doc Holliday's cane, in a gesture of restraint. "We don't want that."...

Frank McLowery and Billy Clanton jerked and fired their six-guns simultaneously. Both turned loose on Wyatt Earp, the shots with which they opened the famous battle of the O.K. Corral echoing from the adobe walls as one.

Fast as the two rustlers were at getting into action from a start with guns half-drawn, Wyatt Earp was deadlier. Frank McLowery's bullet tore through the skirt of Wyatt's coat on the right, Billy Clanton's ripped the marshal's sleeve, but before either could fire again, Wyatt's Buntline Special roared; the slug struck Frank McLowery squarely in the abdomen, just above the belt buckle. McLowery screamed, clapped his left hand to the wound, bent over and staggered forward. Wyatt knew Frank as the most dangerous of the five outlaws and had set out deliberately to dispose of him.

In this fraction of a second, Tom McLowery jumped behind Frank's horse, drawing his gun and shooting under the animal's neck at Morgan Earp. The bullet cut Morgan's coat. Billy Clanton shot a second and a third time at Wyatt, missing with both as Morgan turned loose on him, aiming for Billy's stomach, but hitting the cowboy's gun hand....

Tom McLowery's second slug had hit Morgan Earp in the left shoulder ...[but Morgan] shot Billy in the chest as Virgil put a slug into Clanton's body, just underneath the twelfth rib.

Before Wyatt could throw down on Tom McLowery...Ike Clanton had covered the few feet across the corral and seized Wyatt's left arm.

"Don't kill me, Wyatt! Don't kill me!" the pot-valiant Clanton pleaded. "I'm not shooting!"

"This fight's commenced. Get to fighting or get out," Wyatt answered, throwing Ike off.

Tom McLowery was firing his third shot, this at Wyatt as Ike Clanton hung to the marshal's arm, when Doc Holliday turned loose both barrels of his shotgun simultaneously from the road. Tom's shot went wild and McLowery started on a run around the corner of the assay office toward Third Street. Disgusted with a weapon that could miss at such a range, Holliday hurled the sawed-off shotgun after Tom with an oath and jerked his nickel-plated Colt's. Ten feet around the corner, Tom McLowery fell dead with the double charge of buckshot in his belly and a slug from Wyatt Earp's six-gun under his ribs which had hit him as he ran.

The wounded Frank McLowery was next to die, as Ike Clanton ran away. Virgil Earp was wounded in the leg. Doc Holliday received a flesh wound from a ricocheting bullet. Billy Claiborne ducked out of the fight, hiding behind a building. Billy Clanton was the last to fall.

...The firing ceased. Billy Claiborne ran from the rear of Fly's [Photo Gallery] on through toward Allen Street. Holliday's trigger clicked futilely.

"What in hell did you let Ike Clanton get away like that for, Wyatt?" Doc complained.

"He wouldn't jerk his gun," Wyatt answered.

The fight was over.

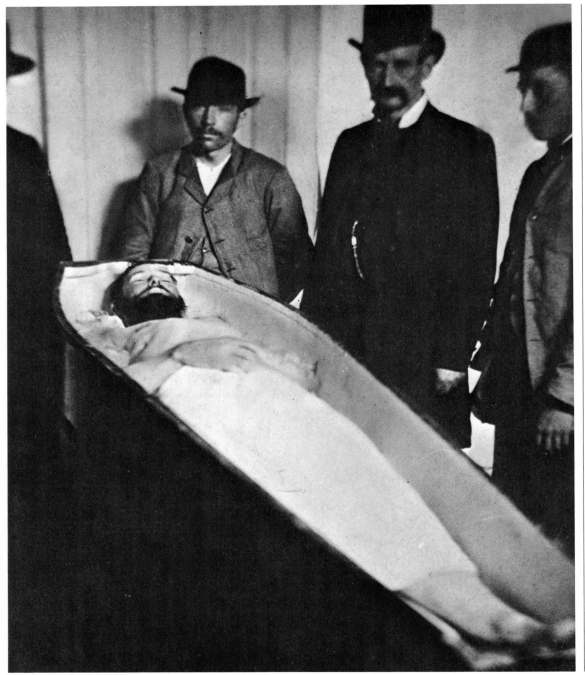

"THE DIRTY LITTLE COWARD WHO SHOT MR. HOWARD HAS LAID POOR JESSE IN HIS GRAVE"

From a sworn account at the coroner's inquest into the death of Jesse James, April 3, 1882:

My name is Robert Ford and I am twenty-one years of age....In January last I had a conversation with Governor Crittenden, the result of which I became a detective to hunt the James outlaws....Governor Crittenden asked me if I thought I could catch Jesse James, and I answered yes....The governor therefore agreed to pay $10,000 apiece for the production of Jesse and Frank James, whether dead or alive. This interview occurred in the St. James Hotel in Kansas City.

I have been with Jesse constantly since last Sunday night....Jesse and I had a talk yesterday about robbing the bank at Platte City (Mo.), and which Charley [a friend] and I both agreed to assist. Between eight and nine o'clock this morning while the three of us were in a room in Jesse's

house, Jesse pulled off his coat and also his pistols, two of which he constantly wore, and then got up onto a chair for the purpose of brushing dust off a picture.

While Jesse was thus engaged, Charley winked at me, so I knew he meant for me to shoot. So, as quickly as possible, I drew my pistol and aiming at Jesse's head, which was not more than four feet from the muzzle of my weapon, I fired, and Jesse tumbled headlong from the chair on which he was standing and fell on his face.

HANGING

Fort Smith, in Indian territory, was the scene of numerous hangings of criminals convicted in the court of the famous "Hanging Judge" Isaac C. Parker. The most celebrated execution was that of longtime outlaw Cherokee Bill, described here by Paul I. Wellman.

Cherokee Bill turned his broad, impassive face, with its gleaming eyes, about and said, "Hell, look at the people; something must be going to happen."

Before the hood was placed over his head he was asked if he had any final word to say.

"No," he replied gruffly. "I came here to die, not to make a speech."

A final prayer was said, the hangman's noose was adjusted, the black cap pulled over his face.

"Move over a little, Bill," said Eoff, his hand on the lever.

Cherokee Bill obediently moved his huge feet until he stood over the center of the trap.

The lever was pulled, his figure shot down through the opening, dropped ten feet, and that was the end. His neck was broken and he died without a struggle.

American Bison (*Bison americanus*).

David R. Miles

THE LIFE
OF
THE TIMES

FREDERIC REMINGTON: *Coming and Going of the Pony Express;* Thomas Gilcrease Institute, Tulsa, Oklahoma.

PONY EXPRESS

In the spring of 1860, a new means of communications between the Midwest and California emerged—the Pony Express. Mark Twain, writing a few years after the service began, describes the Pony Express as he saw it during a trip to Nevada.

The pony rider was usually a little bit of a man, brimful of spirit and endurance. No matter what time of the day or night his watch came on and no matter whether it was winter or summer, raining, snowing, hailing, or sleeting, or whether his beat was a level straight road or a crazy trail over the mountain crags and precipices, or whether it led through peaceful regions or regions that swarmed with hostile Indians, he must always be ready to leap into the saddle and be off like the wind! There was no idling time for a pony rider on duty. He rode fifty miles without stopping, by daylight, moonlight, starlight, or through the blackness of darkness—just as it happened.... And then, as he came crashing up to the station where stood two men holding fast a fresh, impatient steed, the transfer of rider and mailbag was made in the twinkling of an eye, and away flew the eager pair and were out of sight before the spectator could get hardly the ghost of a look.

THE COWBOY'S LAMENT

1. As   I   rode   down   to   La-   re-   do,   La-   re-   do,
Chorus 1: "Just   play   the   fife   slow-   ly   and   beat   the   drum   low-   ly,
4. "Oh,   bring   me a   glass   of   cold   wa-   ter, cold   wa-   ter,

As   I   rode   down   to   La-   re-   do   one   day,
And   play   the   death march   as   you   bear   me   a-   long.
Just   bring   me a   glass   of   cold   wa-   ter," he   said.

I   saw   a   young   cow-   boy   all   dressed   in   white   lin-   en,
Just   take   me   to   Boot Hill   and   chuck   the   sod   o'er   me,
But   when   I   re-turned with   the   glass   of   cold   wa-   ter

All   dressed   in   white   lin-   en   and   cold   as   the   clay.
For   I'm   a   poor   cow-   boy   and I   know   I've   done   wrong.
The   poor   young   cow-   boy   was   dead.

O.C. SELTZER: *The Night Herder's Clock;* Thomas Gilcrease Institute, Tulsa, Oklahoma.

"IRREGULAR" DOCTORS

While some military surgeons and European-trained physicians made their way west in the 1800s, most of the people practicing medicine had learned what they knew not in any school but by chance or necessity, as related here by Richard Dunlop.

At the age of eighteen the redoubtable Kit [Carson] found himself alone in the wilderness with a companion who had a shattered arm. Using only a razor and a handsaw, he amputated the arm. Then he seared the blood vessels with a heated iron bar. Peg-leg Smith did Kit one better. When an Indian bullet mangled his leg, he sat down beneath a tree, ligated his limb with a buckskin thong and amputated with his hunting knife.

Sometimes an authentic M.D. had a run-in with an "irregular" doctor. Here is what happened when Dr. Edward Walters hung out his shingle in Placerville, California—a town already served by a self-styled physician named Hullings.

Although Hullings was generally too drunk even to take the pulse of any man jack who fell ill, they listened sympathetically. Tall and bulky in a black coat, flaunting a Mexican sash about his waist, he strode into Dr. Walters' office with half the town at his heels. He demanded to see the newcomer's diploma and certificate. While the miners jeered at him, Walters got out the documents. Hullings seized the precious papers, ripped them in half and deluged their owner's face with a well-directed jet of tobacco juice.

Fortunately, Dr. Walters had had a liberal education as well as medical training. He called Dr. Hullings out of doors to fight a duel, then plugged him through the heart. His first triumphant act as Placerville's official physician was to sign his rival's death certificate.

ADVERTISING THE COLT

To James Dean Alden,
Colt Agent, Avizon, 1860

I am noticing in the newspapers occasionally complimentary notices of the Sharp & Burnside Rifles & Carbines, anecdotes of their use upon Grisly Bears, Indians, Mexicans, &c.&c. Now this is all wrong—it should be published Colts Rifles, Carbines &c. When there is or can be made a good Story of the use of a Colt's Revolving Rifle, Carbine, Shotgun or Pistol, for publication in *The Arizonian* the opportunity should not be lost, and in the event of such notices being published you must always send me one hundred copies. If there is a chance to do a few good things in this way, give the editor a Pistol or Rifle compliment, in the way it will tell—. You know how to do this & Do not forget to have his Columns report all the accidents that occur to the Sharps & other humbug arms. I hope soon to see the evidence of your usefulness in this line of business.

Samuel Colt

MOUNTAIN MEN COME COURTING

Even the fierce American mountaineers — the trappers and hunters who survived by their strength and wits — came back to "civilization" to find a bride. In the following piece first published in 1849, George F. Ruxton tells of La Bonté and his companions who arrive at Taos, New Mexico.

More than one of the mountaineers had fulfilled the object of their journey, and had taken to themselves a partner from amongst the belles of Taos, and now they were preparing for their return to the mountains. Dick Wooton was the only unfortunate one. He had wooed a damsel whose parents peremptorily forbade their daughter to wed the hunter, and he therefore made ready for his departure with considerable regret.

The day came, however. The band of mountaineers were already mounted, and those with wives in charge were some hours on the road, leaving the remainder quaffing many a stirrup-cup before they left. Dick Wooton was as melancholy as a buffalo bull in spring; and as he rode down the village, and approached the house of his lady-love, who stood wrapped in reboso, and cigarito in mouth, on the sill of the door, he turned away his head as if dreading to say adios. La Bonté rode beside him, and a thought struck him.

"Ho, Dick!" he said, "thar's the gal, and thar's the mountains: shoot sharp's the word."

Dick instantly understood him, and was "himself again." He rode up to the girl as if to bid her adieu, and she came to meet him. Whispering one word, she put her foot upon his, was instantly seized round the waist, and placed upon the horn of his saddle. He struck spurs into his horse, and in a minute was out of sight, his three companions covering his retreat, and menacing with their rifles the crowd which was soon drawn to the spot by the cries of the girl's parents, who had been astonished spectators of the daring rape.

The trapper and his bride, however, escaped scatheless, and the whole party effected a safe passage of the mountains, and reached the Arkansa, where the band was broken up....

SOD HOUSE

The most common dwelling put up by early settlers was the sod house. It was wind- and fire-proof, according to Everett Dick in his book The Sod House Frontier, *but when it rained...*

...Soon little rivulets of muddy water were running through the sleepers' hair. The sod house dweller had to learn to migrate when it rained. If the rain came from the north, the north side of the house leaked, and it was necessary to move everything to the south side, if from the south, a move had to be made again....

One pioneer woman remembered frying pancakes with someone holding an umbrella over her and the stove. A visitor at the home of a Dakota woman said that when great clouds rolled up in the afternoon the lady of the homestead began gathering up all the old dishes in the house and placing them here and there on the floor, on the stove, and on the bed. The visitor remarked that the prairie woman seemed to understand her business for when the rain came down in torrents a few minutes later every drop that came through the numerous holes in the roof of the shack went straight into those vessels. After a heavy rain it was necessary to hang all the bed clothing and wearing apparel on the line to dry.

N.C. WYETH: *A Word of Precaution to the Passengers;*
National Cowboy Hall of Fame and Western Heritage Center, Oklahoma City, Oklahoma.

STAGECOACH

In 1871 Mark Twain published Roughing It, *an account of his experiences in the Far West. He traveled from the Midwest to Carson City, Nevada, by stagecoach, which he depicts as "an imposing cradle on wheels."*

Our coach was a great swinging and swaying stage, of the most sumptuous description—an imposing cradle on wheels. It was drawn by six handsome horses, and by the side of the driver sat the "conductor," the legitimate captain of the craft; for it was his business to take charge and care of the mails, baggage, express matter, and passengers. We three were the only passengers, this trip. We sat on the back seat, inside. About all the rest of the coach was full of mail-bags —for we had three days' delayed mails with us....

We changed horses every ten miles, all day long, and fairly flew over the hard, level road. We jumped out and stretched our legs every time the coach stopped, and so the night found us still vivacious and unfatigued.

After supper a woman got in, who lived about fifty miles further on, and we three had to take turns at sitting outside with the driver and conductor. Apparently she was not a talkative woman. She would sit there in the gathering twilight and fasten her steadfast eyes on a mosquito rooting into her arm, and slowly she would raise her other hand till she had got his range, and then she would launch a slap at him that would have jolted a cow; and after that she would sit and contemplate the corpse with tranquil satisfaction—for she never missed her mosquito; she was a dead shot at short range....

Whenever the stage stopped to change horses, we would wake up, and try to recollect where we were—and succeed—and in a minute or two the stage would be off again, and we likewise. We began to get into country, now, threaded here and there with little streams. These had high, steep banks on each side, and every time we flew down one bank and scrambled up the other, our party inside got mixed somewhat. First we would all be down in a pile at the forward end of the stage, nearly in a sitting posture, and in a second we would shoot to the other end, and stand on our heads. And we would sprawl and kick, too, and ward off ends and corners of mail-bags that came lumbering over us and about us; and as the dust rose from the tumult, we would all sneeze in chorus, and the majority of us would grumble, and probably say some hasty thing, like: "Take your elbow out of my ribs!—can't you quit crowding?"...

At midnight it began to rain, and I never saw anything like it—indeed, I did not even see this, for it was too dark. We fastened down the curtains and even calked them with clothing, but the rain streamed in in twenty places, notwithstanding. There was no escape. If one moved his feet out of a stream, he brought his body under one; and if he moved his body he caught one somewhere else. If he struggled out of the drenched blankets and sat up, he was bound to get one down the back of his neck. Meantime the stage was wandering about a plain with gaping gullies in it, for the driver could not see an inch before his face nor keep the road, and the storm pelted so pitilessly that there was no keeping the horses still. With the first abatement the conductor turned out with lanterns to look for the road, and the first dash he made was into a chasm about fourteen feet deep, his lantern following like a meteor. As soon as he touched bottom he sang out frantically:

"Don't come here!"

To which the driver, who was looking over the precipice where he had disappeared, replied, with an injured air: "Think I'm a dam' fool?"...

We were approaching the end of our long journey. It was the morning of the twentieth day. At noon we would reach Carson City, the capital of Nevada Territory. We were not glad, but sorry. It had been a fine pleasure trip; we had fed fat on wonders every day; we were now well accustomed to stage life, and very fond of it; so the idea of coming to a standstill and settling down to a humdrum existence in a village was not agreeable, but on the contrary depressing.

Visibly our new home was a desert, walled in by barren, snow-clad mountains. There was not a tree in sight. There was no vegetation but the endless sage-brush and greasewood. All nature was gray with it. We were plowing through great deeps of powdery alkali dust that rose in thick clouds and floated across the plain like smoke from a burning house. We were coated with it like millers; so were the coach, the mules, the mail-bags, the driver—we and the sage-brush and the other scenery were all one monotonous color. Long trains of freight-wagons in the distance enveloped in ascending masses of dust suggested pictures of prairies on fire. These teams and their masters were the only life we saw. Otherwise we moved in the midst of solitude, silence, and desolation. Every twenty steps we passed the skeleton of some dead beast of burthen, with its dust-coated skin stretched tightly over its empty ribs....

By and by Carson City was pointed out to us....

We arrived, disembarked, and the stage went on.

THE UNSINKABLE MRS. BROWN

Maggie Tobin was born in Hannibal, Missouri, in 1867. When she was 17 she went to join her brother in the wild mining town of Leadville, Colorado. In 1886 Maggie married James J. Brown. Later they became rich through gold mining and in 1894 moved to Denver. Caroline Bancroft writes of the colorful Mrs. Brown:

Maggie Brown set out to conquer Denver society. She had very little knowledge of money or manners. Her English was atrocious and gave birth to many a story, told with malicious glee at smart dinner parties. Actually Jim Brown had made, and was to make, only a million or two, and his fortune was always much less than many other Colorado and Denver millionaires of this period. But Maggie spent money as if she were married to a Croesus in an effort to make the social grade....

Snubbed repeatedly by those she tried to know, her ambition was undaunted. She hired tutors to teach her English, French, singing, elocution and deportment. She began to travel extensively to Europe and, by the turn of the century, around the world.

Typical of Maggie's style was the time she had some Indians camp on the Capitol grounds as publicity for a charity fair. The legislators and governor, however, forced them to leave.

When Maggie heard the story of their predicament, she refused to be outdone by a few stuffy legislators.

"Hell, you can camp here," she said.

Accordingly the Indians pitched their tents on her front lawn....

The news soon spread about town, and droves of horseless carriages and smart turn-outs were driving up and down Pennsylvania Street to see what the Impossible Mrs. Brown was up to now.

At this juncture Jim Brown returned home. The sight appalled him. He lost his Irish temper, packed his bag and left for Arizona, refusing to return. Undismayed Maggie made a huge success of the Fair, turned the money over to St. Joseph's hospital, rented [her house], and left for the East.

Maggie Brown eventually became accepted in high society everywhere — except Denver. She was one of the survivors of the Titanic.

O.C. SELTZER: *Circuit Rider;*
Thomas Gilcrease Institute, Tulsa, Oklahoma.

67

FRONTIER MINISTER

Badger Clark recalls his father, C.B. Clark, who had his pulpit in a mining camp "which contained five churches, twenty-six saloons and three or four other institutions of very doubtful repute...."

At that time a minister was primarily a preacher, and C.B. could preach. His big, mellow bass needed no amplifying. Its tones had an effect on the nerves something like those of a well-played cello. The sermons were well thought out, with much walking of the floor and looking into books. The only record of them was a few lines of atrocious handwriting on the back of an old envelope. Once he had established sympathetic contact with the audience, he was likely to forget the envelope. His thoughts flowed easily and gracefully into ready phrases. He was enjoying himself. So was his congregation. "I had liberty this morning," he would say. And a parishioner said: "When he has finished, I feel lifted up and, at the same time, ashamed of myself."

CHARLES RUSSELL: *Buffalo Hunt;*
Amon Carter Museum of Western Art, Fort Worth, Texas.

69

"BUFFALO HORSE"

Following the Civil War, General Philip Sheridan, the famous cavalryman, spent time on the western plains where he was impressed by many things, including the "buffalo horse."

There is something majestic and formidable in the appearance of a buffalo. It is therefore not surprising that but few horses will readily approach sufficiently near to enable the hunter to make a close shot. Some horses rebel, notwithstanding every effort to allay their alarm. Others, by a proper course of training, carry their riders, without any direction, into just the position desirable. Such an animal is a treasure in the esteem of a plainsman. He talks about his "buffalo horse" with more pride than he would of himself, had he accomplished a feat ever so wonderful.

WILLIAM R. LEIGH: *Buffalo;*
Thomas Gilcrease Institute, Tulsa, Oklahoma.

SAN FRANCISCO: THE BARBARY COAST

A view of the Golden Gate City from the San Francisco Chronicle, *November 28, 1869.*

The Barbary Coast! That mysterious region so much talked of; so seldom visited! Of which so much is heard, but little seen! That sink of moral pollution, whose reefs are strewn with human wrecks, and into whose vortex are constantly drifting barks of mortal life, while swiftly down the whirlpool of death go the sinking hulks of the murdered and the suicide! The Barbary Coast! The stamping ground of the Ranger, the last resort of the ruined *nymphe du pave,* the home of vice and harbor of destruction! The coast on which no gentle breezes blow, but where rages one wild sirocco of sin!

SHEEPMAN

Disputes over land were common in the early West, especially between sheepmen and cattlemen. The so-called "range wars" were mostly bluffs and threats, however, and a sharp sheepman could generally hold his territory, as recorded by Roy Holt.

Sometimes it was necessary to call a cowman's bluff and stand on one's rights. One sheepman in the South Concho country, ordered off the range by a swaggering cowman, was given his choice between three days to move and death at the end of a rope. The sheepman drew a map of the territory around his sheep camp and sent it off to Austin to find out to whom the land belonged. The answer was that, with the exception of four hundred acres some miles away from his camp, it belonged to the State of Texas. The infinitesimal tract excepted belonged to the cowman, and it was all that did belong to him. The next time he came around for a settlement the sheepman told him what he had found out. He added that if there were any more trouble he would arrange to have fifty thousand sheep brought in within three months. There was no more trouble.

GO WEST, YOUNG MAN!

The famed newspaper editor Horace Greeley was on a trip through the West in 1859 when he heard about a gold discovery in Colorado. He went to see it with his own eyes. Alice Polk Hill reveals how some folks in Denver decided to play a little joke on Mr. Greeley.

The boys took down an old shotgun and fired gold dust into a hole for all it was worth.

Bright and early the next morning a spanking team was rigged up, and the distinguished gentleman started for the gulch, accompanied by some of the most plausible, entertaining and versatile talkers of the country. They escorted him over the diggings, related all the interesting events in the history of its discovery, showed him specimens of the dirt and the pure gold that had been washed out. Mr. Greeley's soul was in arms, and, eager for the task, he called for a shovel and pan, rolled up his sleeves, and went down into the pit. They gave him all the necessary instructions as to the process of panning, and looked on with palpitating anxiety.

Horace Greeley

Mr. Greeley was an apt scholar, and put his dirt through like an adept in the art. It panned out big. All the bottom of the pan was covered with bright gold particles. They slapped him on the shoulders in regular Western style, and told him to try it again — which he did — with the same success. Then he gathered up his gold dust in a bag, and said:

"Gentlemen, I have worked with my own hands and seen with my own eyes, and the news of your rich discovery shall go all over the world, as far as my paper can waft it."

Mr. Greeley left, believing he had made a thorough test. As soon as he reached New York he devoted a whole side of the *Tribune* to an ecstatic description of the camp, headed with large, glaring type, such as "bill-stickers" use. The report was read all over the country, and caused a great rush to the land of promise. Those who had the fever took a relapse, and they had it bad. It was a raging epidemic, and spread faster than the cholera in Egypt.

He shouted into the ears of the over-crowded East until the welkin rang, "Young man, go West!" It was his glowing articles and earnest advice about "going West" that caused the first great boom in Colorado. The honest old man went down to his grave ignorant of the joke that was played upon him.

EAST MEETS WEST

On May 10, 1869, the "golden spike" was driven at Promontory, Utah, which linked the railway east and west. The reminiscences of Alexander Toponce recall the event.

On the last day, only about 100 feet were laid, and everybody tried to have a hand in the work. I took a shovel from an Irishman, and threw a shovel full of dirt on the ties just to tell about it afterward....

When they came to drive the last spike, Governor Stanford, president of the Central Pacific, took the sledge, and the first time he struck he missed the spike and hit the rail.

What a howl went up! Irish, Chinese, Mexicans, and everybody yelled with delight. "He missed it. Yee." The engineers blew the whistles and rang their bells. Then Stanford tried it again and tapped the spike and the telegraph operators had fixed their instruments so that the tap was reported in all the offices east and west, and set bells to tapping in hundreds of towns and cities....

It was a great occasion, every one carried off souvenirs and there are enough splinters of the last tie in museums to make a good bonfire.

IRON HORSE

In the fall of 1879 Robert Louis Stevenson traveled by train across the United States, writing of the trip:

Mile upon mile, and not a tree, a bird, or a river. Only down the long, sterile canyons the train shot hooting and awoke the resting echo. That train was the one piece of life in all the deadly land; it was the one actor, the one spectacle fit to be observed in this paralysis of man and nature. And when I think how the railroad has been pushed through this unwatered wilderness and haunt of savage tribes...how at each stage of the construction roaring, impromptu cities, full of gold and lust and death, sprang up and then died away...how in these uncouth places pigtailed Chinese pirates worked side by side with border ruffians and broken men from Europe, talking together in a mixed dialect...and then when I go on to remember that all this epical turmoil was conducted by gentlemen in frock coats and with a view to nothing more extraordinary than a fortune and a subsequent visit to Paris, it seems to me, I own, as if this railway were the one typical achievement of the age in which we live, as if it brought together into one plot all the ends of the world and all the degrees of social rank, and offered to some great writer the busiest, the most extended, and the most varied subject for an enduring literary work. If it be romance, if it be contrast, if it be heroism that we require, what was Troy town to this?

THOMAS MORAN: *Acoma;*
Thomas Gilcrease Institute, Tulsa, Oklahoma.

OUT WHERE THE WEST BEGINS

Out where the handclasp's a little stronger,
Out where the smile dwells a little longer,
　　That's where the West begins;
Out where the sun is a little brighter,
Where the snows that fall are a trifle whiter,
Where the bonds of home are a wee bit tighter,
　　That's where the West begins.

Out where the skies are a trifle bluer,
Out where friendship's a little truer,
　　That's where the West begins;
Out where a fresher breeze is blowing,
Where there's laughter in every streamlet flowing,
Where there's more of reaping and less of sowing,
　　That's where the West begins.

Out where the world is in the making,
Where fewer hearts in despair are aching,
　　That's where the West begins;
Where there's more of singing and less of sighing,
Where there's more of giving and less of buying,
And a man makes friends without half trying,
　　That's where the West begins.

Arthur Chapman

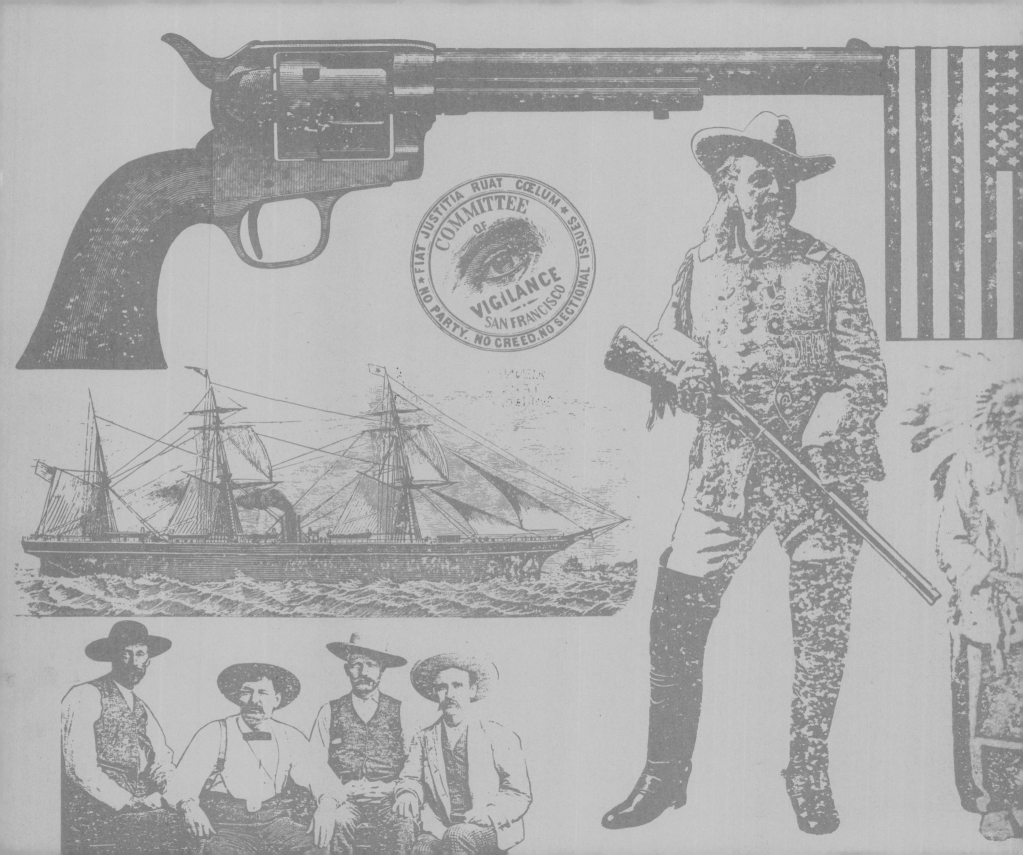